THE FIRST BOOK OF JAZZ

THE FIRST BOOK OF

JAZZ

LANGSTON HUGHES

UPDATED EDITION
FRANKLIN WATTS
NEW YORK
LONDON
1976

Photographs courtesy of: Nigerian Information Service: p. 5; Culver Pictures, Inc.: frontispiece, pp. 6, 44; The Association for the Study of Afro-American Life and History, Inc.: p. 11; New Orleans Jazz Museum: pp. 15, 16, 19, 34; CBS Records: pp. 20, 39, 54; RCA Records: frontispiece, p. 24; Museum of the City of New York, Theater and Music Collection: p. 27; The Museum of Modern Art/Film Stills Archive: pp. 30, 48; Charles Stewart: frontispiece, pp. 51, 57.

Cover design by Paul Gamarello

Library of Congress Cataloging in Publication Data

Hughes, Langston, 1902–1967.
      The first book of jazz.

      (A First book)
      Includes index.
      SUMMARY: An introduction to jazz, focusing on its historical development and its most famous performers.
      1. Jazz music—Juvenile literature. [1. Jazz music] I. Title.
ML3561.J3H84   1976   785.4'2   76–39
ISBN 0–531–00565–8

CONTENTS

THE FIRST BOOK OF JAZZ

JUST FOR FUN

When little Louis Armstrong, who was born on the Fourth of July, 1900, started singing for pennies on street corners in New Orleans, he was about seven years old. Before he was twelve, with Happy, Little Mack, and Georgie, he formed a quartet. Louis sang bass and sometimes whistled through his fingers like a clarinet. The four boys would move up and down Perdido Street harmonizing beneath people's windows in the evening. But sometimes, instead of having coins showered down upon them, they would be angrily chased away. Louis thought maybe a guitar would help their music, and be more fun, too. So he made himself a sort of ukulele from a cigar box. He did this by nailing a flat piece of wood to the box for a neck, then stringing some wire from the neck tightly across the open side of the box.

The other boys probably put together homemade instruments for themselves, too, so that for fun they all could have a band. Maybe the only thing they bought was a five-and-ten-cent-store mouth organ for Little Mack. As many boys in the South have done, Happy found an old tin washtub somewhere and made himself a bass viol. Georgie borrowed his mother's washboard. He put thimbles on the ends of his fingers and stroked the washboard to play a rhythm. Maybe Mack played a little blues tune on his harmonica that he learned by ear.

So we can imagine the four boys together in the backyard under a chinaberry tree, playing at music. Louis picked the strings of his cigar box and sang, Happy plunked at his washtub bass, Little Mack blew his harmonica, and Georgie stroked gaily on his washboard. After a while they made such a happy beat that the other children in the neighborhood came running to sing and dance to their playing. Their band was fun.

Many young people have made such washboard bands by putting together their own instruments. Some of these bands have even been recorded by the big record companies. In New Orleans, before Louis was born, there was a band that is still written about in books today. A blind newsboy (or "newsie") whose nickname was Stale Bread started a little street-corner band with homemade instruments. Perhaps one of his players had a washboard. Maybe another shook two spoons together like minstrel bones. Maybe one newsie used a box for a drum, and perhaps another had a mouth organ. At any rate, they made such lively music that sometimes all of them would start jigging as they played. They shook their shoulders and bobbed their heads as if they had St. Vitus's dance. At the same time they let their feet fly so frantically that folks started calling them the Spasm Band. From that time on, throughout the South such washboard bands were called spasm bands.

Young folks — like the newsboy Stale Bread of long ago — still put together such bands — mainly in small towns and country places. In the Tennessee mountains, sometimes their leader blows into a jug and the band is called a jug band. Or sometimes, instead of a mouth organ, maybe a tin whistle or a kazoo is used. Tunes are also played on a comb with a thin piece of paper over it. A dishpan may be used for a drum. There is never any written music. The tunes are remembered or made up as the players play. And, to the players, it is play — just for fun. That is how the music called jazz began — with people playing for fun.

AFRICAN DRUMS AND OLD NEW ORLEANS

Something to beat on, thump on, or stroke on has always been a part of play-music — often the only part — for a beat or a rhythm is as important as a tune, sometimes more important. Maybe that is because hundreds of years ago music began with rhythm. Men would beat on a hollow log, then sing; or they would beat on a goatskin drum and dance. Ancient peoples everywhere, in Europe and Asia and Africa, beat on things to make a rhythm. The Indians in America beat on drums as they danced. Some people in some parts of the world — in the South Seas, the West Indies, and Africa — still make music just by beating on drums. In parts of Africa there are whole orchestras made up of nothing but drums — big drums and little drums, tall drums and short drums, dull drums and deep drums. Each drummer may play a different rhythm, but all the rhythms are so woven together that people can sing or dance to them.

For centuries, folks in West Africa have worked to

rhythm, rowed boats to rhythm, pounded their meal to rhythm, and built their houses to rhythm. Then, when they were tired of working, they danced to the rhythms of their drums. They shook little rattles made of gourds, rang bells, and clapped their hands to add to the rhythm. Often Africans have many different rhythms going all at once — kinds that people nowhere else in the world can play. But all of them are woven together into a happy sound that makes folks want to get up and move in time to the rhythms. When the Africans first came to the New World, more than four hundred years ago, they brought these wonderful rhythms with them. One important thing that makes American jazz different from the music of other countries is that it is full of a variety of rhythms. In part, jazz grew out of the beating of African drums. The drum is our basic rhythm instrument.

Old New Orleans

A hundred and fifty years ago in old New Orleans there was a public square called Congo Square. It was a big wide open dusty place. On Sundays, when they did not have to work, the African slaves went there with their drums to sing and dance what they called the bamboula. Crowds used to gather around the square to watch the dancing slaves and listen to the music that they made on their drums. This was mostly rhythm music. But sometimes the dancers began to sing or to chant African songs they remembered against the drums. Sometimes they made up words of their own.

Some people who write about the history of American jazz believe that jazz began in New Orleans, where the bands and orchestras borrowed some of the rhythms of the

JAZZ HAS BORROWED ITS RHYTHMS
FROM THE BEATING OF AFRICAN DRUMS.

HERE A BRASS BAND,
ORGANIZED BY TENANT FARMERS,
BEATS OUT A JAZZ TUNE.

drums in Congo Square. The rhythms that the drummers beat out in the dusty sunlight made the people standing around want to move their heads in time, tap their feet, and dance. That is one of the things about jazz: it always makes people want to move. Jazz music is music to move to — not just to listen to.

The African drummers in New Orleans did not have any written music. They played from memory or made up rhythms as they went along. They were playing just for fun. Today the best jazz is often played from a tune that is remembered. It is played as one feels like playing it — for fun at that particular moment.

New Orleans had been a French and a Spanish city before it became American. So, in addition to the slave drums, it knew many different kinds of music, both popular and classical. There was a great opera house in New Orleans long before the Civil War. And there were very fine orchestras and bands in the Louisiana city. But many people could not afford to go to the opera house, or listen to the symphony orchestras, or learn to play music by note as trained musicians did. So the poor people, without teachers, made their own music, playing mostly by ear. For fun, they played the melodies of old Spanish songs and French dance quadrilles. They put behind them the beat of the Congo Square drums.

Old New Orleans had many marching bands that played a louder, livelier, more steadily rhythmical music than orchestras in opera houses or concert halls. People almost danced when they marched behind such bands. On the sidewalks, children did dance. When Louis Armstrong's parents were young, these brass bands often played in the streets or in parks where everybody could hear them without paying. The sidewheel steamers that paddled up and down the Mississippi River from New Orleans to Memphis and St. Louis carried little bands on them. So the lively drum-time marching music of New Orleans, many years ago, began to spread through the heart of America. And it turned into dancing music. Its syncopated 1–2–3–4 beat (a particular kind of 1–2–3–4 beat played with the accent shifted to the weak beat and stepped up a bit by memories of Congo Square) became a part of jazz.

Of course, people were making music in other parts of our country — not just in New Orleans. In New England, settlers were singing their hymns. In Virginia and Kentucky, the newcomers were singing their ballads. In the Far West, the Indians were playing on their drums. African slaves in Georgia, the Carolinas, and other parts of the South, who did not always have drums on which to play, were making up songs to chop cotton to, load the riverboats, or build the levees. They made up field hollers with long, sad, wailing blue notes in their voices that said how tired a man can be. The blacks were also making up religious songs, called spirituals, with the rhythms of the drums in their voices. All of this — the singing, the tunes, and the rhythms — from New England to New Orleans has made American music what it is. A part of American music is jazz, born in the South. Woven into it in the Deep South were the rhythms of African drums that today make jazz music different from any other music in the world. Nobody else ever made jazz before we did. Jazz is American music.

WORK SONGS, JUBILEES AND SPIRITUALS

At the turpentine plant where he worked, little Louis Armstrong's father sometimes sang at his job. The stevedores (people who load and unload ships) on the New Orleans docks sang as they lifted their heavy loads. Today, in some parts of Africa, women pound corn for meal by putting the corn on a flat stone on the ground and beating it with another stone. As the American Indians used to do, these African women carry their babies tied on their backs. As they mash the corn they sing, and the stone in each woman's hand strikes the other stone in rhythm. As a mother's back bends and rises, the baby on her back feels the steady rhythm of this pounding of the corn.

Work songs, all around the world, are full of rhythm. The "Song of the Volga Boatmen" was sung when people pulled barges up rivers in old Russia. Woodsmen everywhere sing tree-chopping songs. Harvest songs for the cutting of grain are thousands of years old. On boats, sailors sang sea chanteys when they raised a boat's sails. And on the Mississippi River, slaves sang while they loaded cotton bales. Some of the rhythms of Afro-American work songs went into the making of jazz. "John Henry" is an American railroad-building song, sung as the picks of rock-crushing hammers struck the rock to clear the way for a roadbed or a tunnel:

Ain't no hammer — huh!
In this mountain — huh!
Rings like mine, boys! — huh!
Rings like mine — huh!

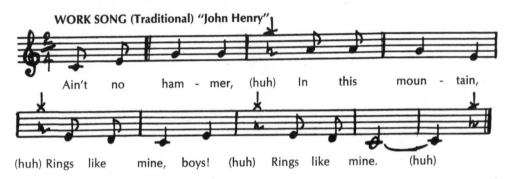

WORK SONG (Traditional) "John Henry"

Ain't no ham - mer, (huh) In this moun - tain,

(huh) Rings like mine, boys! (huh) Rings like mine. (huh)

Many people who were not railroad builders liked this song and would sing or play it just for fun — not to work by. So the "huh" of the hammer's falling was dropped out. Many different people learned this song in different ways. Many singers added verses that they made up. So "John Henry" became a folk song with hundreds of different verses, sung in a great many different ways in different parts of the country. Some of the lines from English ballads got into it, like:

Who's gonna glove your
Pretty little hand?
And who's gonna shoe
Your feet?

But it always kept its work-song rhythm. A part of that rhythm, like the rhythms of many other Southern work songs, became a part of American jazz.

PEOPLE SANG TO THE RHYTHM OF THEIR
WORK—NO MATTER WHAT KIND IT WAS.
THESE WORK SONGS BECAME A PART
OF JAZZ AS WE KNOW IT TODAY.

Jubilees

When Louis Armstrong was a boy, his relatives often sang religious tunes, and sometimes they made up their own words to go with the old melodies. Everywhere, all over the world, people have made up songs about their God, and about the wonders and mysteries of life. The early settlers brought their own hymns from England to the New World and the slaves listened to them. But the African slaves in the American South had to learn a new language: English. So, in their new language, they made up new songs. These songs were called spirituals and were made with English words, a mingling of melodies and harmonies, and African rhythms. But most spirituals had in them a more definite and lively rhythm than English hymns:

> **I got a harp!**
> **You got a harp!**
> **All God's children got a harp!**
> **When I get to heaven**
> **Gonna play on my golden harp —**
> **Play all over God's heaven!**
> **Heaven! Heaven!**
> **Everybody talk about**
> **Heaven ain't going there!**
> **Play all over God's heaven!**

SPIRITUAL "All God's Chillun Got Shoes"

I got a harp! You got a harp! All God's children got a harp!

Spirituals

Some of this rhythm from the spirituals went into the making of jazz.

The spirituals were sometimes called sorrow songs because many of them were about the sadness of life for men and women who were not free:

Nobody knows the trouble I've seen,
Nobody knows but Jesus. . . .

But many spirituals were very lively, too — even though they were religious songs. Some — jubilees — were about the time when freedom would come:

This is the day of jubilee!
God's gonna build up Zion's walls!
The Lord done set His people free!
God's gonna build up Zion's walls!

On a cold autumn day in 1871, eleven students (some of them had been slaves) started out from Fisk University in Tennessee. They were trying to raise some money for their college. Singing their songs of jubilee, four ragged boys and five girls headed northward on a tour. They did not dream then that people would like their songs so well that it would be seven years before they got back to school. These young Fisk Jubilee Singers carried the spirituals over almost all of America and Europe. They sang in little churches and great halls. They sang before Queen Victoria. They sent back $150,000 to their university. And the rhythms of their jubilee songs became more than ever a part of the music of America, later influencing jazz. Jazz has in it some of the qualities of the spirituals.

Minstrel Songs

While the Fisk Jubilee Singers were touring, a black man named James A. Bland wrote a song in the rhythm of the spirituals called "Oh, Dem Golden Slippers":

Oh, dem golden slippers!
Oh, dem golden slippers!
Golden slippers I'm gwinter wear
Because dey look so neat.
Oh, dem golden slippers!
Oh, dem golden slippers!
Golden slippers I'm gwinter wear
To walk de golden streets.

It was not a spiritual. It was a minstrel song, for James Bland was a minstrel man. He toured America and Europe singing his own songs with minstrel shows. Later on, in England, King Edward VII often came to hear him.

From about 1840, and for more than sixty years, the minstrel shows, made up entirely of men, were America's most popular entertainment. For these, such famous songs as "Dixie," "Turkey in the Straw," "Oh, Susannah," and "Old Folks at Home" were written. Most of the minstrel songs were based on African rhythms and melodies borrowed from the work songs and the spirituals. The greatest of the minstrel writers, Stephen Foster, who was white, at first called his songs "Ethiopian" — meaning songs of dark-skinned people. The minstrel shows also made popular the sand dances, the cakewalk, and the plantation jigs that later merged into tap-dancing. Minstrel music featured the tambourines of Europe (similar to the African finger drums)

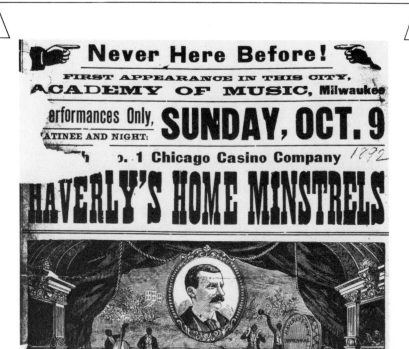

Never Here Before!

FIRST APPEARANCE IN THIS CITY,

ACADEMY OF MUSIC, Milwaukee

erformances Only, **SUNDAY, OCT. 9**

ATINEE AND NIGHT:

o. 1 Chicago Casino Company *1892*

HAVERLY'S HOME MINSTRELS

Under the Immediate Supervision of J. H. HAVERLY, Director, and WM. FOOTE, Manager.

ond all Doubt The Most Comical, Talented and Refined Organization in the World

T OF HAPPY COMEDIANS! A GALAXY OF GREAT SPECIALTIES!

A Colossal Chorus of Choice Vocalists and a Superb Orchestra of Wondrous Ability!

Change of Programme and Performers Presented for the First Tim

SAN FRANCISCO MINSTRELS
NEW OPERA HOUSE
BROADWAY, CORNER 29th STREET.
Opposite the Sturtevant and Gilsey Hotels.

THE MOST BEAUTIFUL, MOST COMPLETE & BEST VENTILATED THEATRE IN THE CITY

MONDAY, Feb. 8th, 1875, and During the Week

ORGANIZED IN 1854!

BIRCH WAMBOLD & BACKUS

20 YEARS OF SUCCESS!

SAN FRANCISCO
MINSTRELS

GLORIOUS SUCCESS OF THE NEW FAIRY TRICK PANTOMIME, ENTITLED

CENTENNIAL! | 1776 & 1876
AS YOU WERE & AS YOU ARE!

BY THE BUTLER PANTOMIME TROUPE

The Trouble begins at 8.   Street Cars may be ordered at 10 o'clock.

MORAL—"GO EARLY."

ENTERTAINMENT A LA SALON
PART PREMIERE.

OVERTURE, arranged by W. S. Mullaly .... SAN FRANCISCO MINSTRELS
BALLAD, "Down among the Blue-Bells" .... MR. EUGENE TREMAIN
COMIC DITTY, "Little Tommy Knox" .... MR. CHARLEY BACKUS
BALLAD, "You never Miss the Water till the Well runs Dry" .... MR. D. S. WAMBOLD
COMIC REFRAIN, "Old Grimes's Cellar Door" .... MR. BILLY BIRCH
BALLAD, "We Sat by the River" .... MR. CARL RUDOLPH
FINALE, Grand Medley .... SAN FRANCISCO MINSTRELS

PART SECOND. "The Virginians" by Thackeray
BETSY AND I ARE OUT, ... WILSON!

along with the banjos and bones of the black plantation bands. The bones were at first two ribs of a sheep or some other small animal. They were polished, held in the hand, and shaken to make a dancing rhythm. Minstrel music borrowed heavily from the black music of the Deep South. A great deal of the minstrel spirit carried over into jazz.

JAZZ FORMS

The Blues

Opening strains of "St. Louis Blues"

BLUES TEMPO

I   hate   to   see   de   evenin' sun   go   down. . . .

I hate to see de evenin' sun go down —

This is the opening of W. C. Handy's famous "St. Louis Blues." Handy, who is called the "father of the blues," was the leader of Mahara's Minstrels in the 1890s. He also played a cornet. And as a trained musician, he could read and write music. Nobody really knows just when, where, or how the kind of songs called blues began. But in 1909 W. C. Handy put down on paper and in 1912 published the "Memphis Blues" (originally called "Mr. Crump"). This was the first of many of his blues songs to become famous. They were based on the melodies and memories of the South, where he was born. In 1914 W. C. Handy's "St. Louis Blues" was published. It has become known all over the world as one of America's most popular songs.

A hundred years ago there were croons, work songs, and field hollers — a kind of musical cry — whose melodies had a blues sound. To these tunes, road workers or cotton pickers put whatever words came into their minds. They sang out their own personal thoughts or sorrows. Maybe somebody in the Deep South, long ago, started to make up a song that began with a kind of field holler. Perhaps, one day while working in a rice field, somebody thought of this song:

Oh, the sun is so hot and the day is so doggone long . . .
Yes, the sun is so hot and the day is so doggone long . . .
And that is the reason I'm singing this doggone song.

Something like that must have happened the day the first blues song was born. For that is the pattern of the blues: a twelve-bar musical pattern — one long line of four bars which is repeated, then a third line of four bars to rhyme with the first two lines that are always the same. Their melody and beat are like those of a field holler. Perhaps thousands of blues were made up in the fields or on the levees, to relieve the monotony of working and to express some thought passing through the singer's mind, or just for fun. One day in Memphis, W. C. Handy wrote down his first blues. Then he and others began to use the blues as a basis for written music. Later a great singer, Bessie Smith, sang

W. C. HANDY—
THE "FATHER OF THE BLUES"

BESSIE SMITH WAS A
FAMOUS BLUES SINGER.

the blues all over the country. She made many records. Now the blues are a part of American jazz.

Jazz took several things from the blues. It often uses the twelve-bar pattern of the blues. And it uses the "blue notes." These blue notes are "off notes" — just a little bit flat and in between the usual notes. They most often are a somewhat flatted third or seventh note of the scale. They are impossible to show in written music, although they are sometimes indicated as flatted notes. But good blues players and singers always sound the blue notes, sliding in with the wailing slurring tones of a real blues song.

Blues also introduced melodies written around five notes only. Using blue notes and various note combinations, whole blues songs were written around five notes. Often, instrumental blues also used "riffs" (single rhythmic phrases repeated over and over, as a background to the melody, or as the melody itself). Jazz today uses riffs. It also uses "breaks," which came from the blues. A break is a little pause at the end of a phrase of melody. During this pause one or more instruments break away from the melody and make up some fill-in music. Breaks are a part of today's jazz, but W. C. Handy's "Memphis Blues" introduced to published music the first printed jazz break of all:

"Memphis Blues"

FIRST PRINTED JAZZ BREAK

The blues are almost always sad songs about being out of work, broke, hungry, far away from home, wanting to get on a train but having no ticket, or being lonely when someone you love has gone. Their music says:

When you see me laughing,
I'm laughing to keep from crying.

And often there is something about the blues that makes people laugh:

I'm going down to the railroad
And lay my head on the track,
Down to the railroad
And lay my head on the track —
But if I see the train a-coming,
I'm gonna jerk it back.

But behind the sadness there is almost always laughter and strength in the blues. Perhaps these qualities make people all around the world love jazz.

Ragtime

The first piano made in America was built in 1775. But for a long time pianos were very expensive. It was not until almost a hundred years later, when several piano-making companies had been formed, that many Americans could afford pianos. Then they became almost as common as radios are today. In the evenings, whole families would take turns playing the piano and would sing for fun.

Poor blacks, newly freed from slavery, often did not have the money to study music, but many learned to play by ear. These black players transferred the rhythms of their drums, their work songs, their cakewalks, and their spirituals to the piano. By the late 1800s they had created a kind of music that came to be called ragtime. This meant playing a piece on the piano in a lively syncopated manner — literally "tearing a tune to tatters." In syncopation the rhythmical accent falls on a beat that would customarily be weak, rather than on a usually strong beat. In ragtime such syncopation ran all the way through each piece. This syncopated ragtime piano style, along with the earlier syncopation of the marching bands, was carried over into jazz. In Sedalia, Missouri, a black musician named Scott Joplin wrote a piece called the "Maple Leaf Rag" in this lively style. It was published in St. Louis in 1899. This happy rag became very popular, and hundreds of other such pieces were written and published. In those days, before the wide use of record players, piano music was recorded on paper rolls and played mechanically on player pianos. Many thousands of ragtime rolls, as well as sheet music, were sold.

One of the great ragtime and blues pianists was a Creole from Louisiana named Jelly Roll Morton. Little Louis Armstrong, as he passed the cafés along Rampart or Basin streets, sometimes listened outside their doors, fascinated by the playing of Mr. Jelly Roll. Jelly Roll sometimes played on the Mississippi riverboats, and at other times he traveled all over the South engaging in piano battles and usually winning the prizes. In the early 1900s he was known from the Mississippi delta to St. Louis, and later all over the country. He played a thousand pianos in as many different towns. In 1938 Jelly Roll Morton spent almost two months in Wash-

JELLY ROLL MORTON   FATS WALLER

ington recording his ragtime and blues for the Folk Archives of the Library of Congress. Younger black piano players like Fats Waller, Willie "The Lion" Smith, and James P. Johnson in New York learned a great deal from Morton. Sometimes these men would all get together and try to outplay each other. In New York's Harlem such battles of music were called cutting contests. Other piano players, from New York's Broadway, listened to these contests in Harlem, and learned from them. Thus this style of piano playing spread and greatly influenced American jazz music.

Boogie-woogie

"Boogie-woogie"
BOOGIE TEMPO

"Trilling the treble and rolling the bass" is the way some players describe "boogie-woogie." Boogie-woogie is a kind of blues-ragtime played on the piano with a strong deep powerful rolling bass added. The left hand pounds out this steady marching bass while the right hand plays a lacework of blues over the bass, often in another rhythm. One hand makes the piano a talking drum. The other hand makes it a singing voice.

The rhythms of boogie-woogie may be traced back to the plantation banjo and the minstrel shouts. But it was not until about 1930 that a long, tall tap dancer named Pine Top

Smith first made boogie-woogie on the piano popular in the Middle West. A little later another black pianist in Chicago, Jimmy Yancey, made up a piece on his piano called "Five O'Clock Blues." This became so well known that some people started calling all boogie-woogie music the "fives." Others call it "eight-to-the-bar," because the rolling bass consists of eight eighth-notes in each bar. Chicago and Kansas City were boogie-woogie centers. Some of the best players — Meade Lux Lewis, Albert Ammons, Dan Burley, and Pete Johnson — were well known in those cities before they traveled widely over the country and their music became part of jazz.

SINGING TRUMPETS

The trumpet sounds within-a my soul!
I ain't got long to stay here. . . .

says the old spiritual "Swing Low, Sweet Chariot."
Another spiritual says:

When the lamb-ram-sheep horns begin to blow,
Trumpets begin to sound,
Joshua commanded the children to shout
And the walls came tumbling down!

In the 1890s pianos were not a part of early New Orleans jazz bands. Horns were their main instruments — par-

HORNS — CORNETS AND TRUMPETS —
WERE THE MAIN INSTRUMENTS IN THE
EARLY NEW ORLEANS JAZZ BANDS.

ticularly the short cornet or the slightly longer trumpet. Perhaps there were no pianos used because the earliest jazz bands developed from brass bands. These marching bands could be heard playing for blocks. In those days Buddy Bolden, one of the great horn blowers, would get up on the bandstand and turn loose with a raggy blues on his gleaming trumpet to let people know a dance was taking place in Lincoln Park. People could hear him for many, many blocks and they would begin heading for the dance. To this day New Orleans jazz is usually loud, and the horns top all other instruments.

Long before the days of radio or television, promoters of boxing matches, excursions, or dances often hired bands. The bands would go about in horse-drawn wagons through the streets of New Orleans to advertise these events. Sometimes one band wagon would meet another. Then each would try to see which could outplay the other. They often tied up traffic at the street corners with their wagons. They called these contests cutting contests — a name borrowed later by the jazz piano players in New York City's Harlem.

So that the slide trombone might not hit the other players in the head, these wagon players let the trombonist sit on the floor at the end of the wagon with his feet hanging over the tailgate. From this custom comes the name "tailgate" for a style of jazz trombone playing that originated in New Orleans.

Sometimes a rich young man would hire one of these wagons full of musicians to serenade his sweetheart. Then people called them serenade wagons. Of course, the band played softly and sweetly for a serenade. But most of the time, in a wagon or not, for dances, picnics, parades, commercials, or even for funerals, the sounding brasses of these old bands could be heard for blocks.

A horde of children always followed these marching bands through the streets. Dancing along or playing on their own homemade instruments while keeping time with the music, these youngsters were called the "second line." As a "second liner," young Louis Armstrong followed such bands through the streets and fell in love with their wonderful horns. As he grew up, he began to dream of playing a singing trumpet himself.

LOUIS ARMSTRONG

The story of Louis Armstrong is almost the whole story of orchestral jazz in America. His life stretched from the very beginnings of such jazz in New Orleans until the 1970s. Louis Armstrong took jazz almost everywhere on earth. He was very famous. But when he was a little boy in New Orleans plunking his music-cigar-box, he was sometimes so ragged that if anybody gave him a penny he had to put it in his mouth — he didn't have pockets. Since he had such a big mouth, his playmates called him "Dippermouth," and later, "Satchelmouth." His nickname was "Satchmo'."

Even as a small boy Louis always had a strong, deep, gravelly voice. Maybe that is why, when he was seven years

THE FAMOUS
LOUIS "SATCHELMOUTH" ARMSTRONG

old, he was able to get a job as a newsboy on one of the busiest corners in New Orleans. Louis could be heard for a long way yelling, "Times-Picayune! Times-Picayune!" And later he got a job on a coal wagon crying, "Coal! Coal! A bucket of coal!" But he always wanted to play a horn, like Buddy Bolden, though he was too poor to buy one. It wasn't until he was sent to a reform school, for firing a pistol in the street (on New Year's Eve, 1913), that he got his wish.

At first little Louis played a tambourine in the black Waifs' Band. Later he beat a mighty roll on a small drum in their favorite concert piece, "At the Animals' Ball." Then he became the school bugler. But Louis was in the home almost a year before he was at last entrusted with a trumpet. When the bandmaster finally gave it to him, Louis was so happy that he kissed it. Then he took it to the toolshop and filed notches in its mouthpiece so that it would fit his lips better. Louis became such a good trumpet player that when the Waif's Band was permitted to march in parades outside of the school, everybody along the streets would listen to him.

After two years at the Waifs' Home, Louis was sent back to his parents. He had made up his mind to be a musician although he had to leave the trumpet at the home. He went to work on a coal wagon again. But on Sundays Louis spent the whole day in Lincoln Park or Johnson Park listening to bands. From the old marching bands, little dance bands had now been formed. Louis often begged for a chance to pass out handbills announcing their dances, so that he might get free passes into the halls. One night his mother pulled Louis out of a dance hall by the scruff of his neck and thrashed him good for being away from home so long. But even at home in bed, sometimes Louis could hear Bunk Johnson's cornet blowing the "Twelfth Street Rag," or the cornet king, Joe Oliver, holding the last high notes of the "Tiger Rag." He dreamed of the day when he, too, would play so beautifully. But Louis did not have a horn.

Then one night when he was about sixteen years old, the cornet player in a little café band near Louis's home fell ill. The owner of the café sent for Louis. When he found out that the boy did not have a horn, he bought him a battered old pawnshop cornet for fifteen dollars. Louis started playing with the band that very night. He had not blown a horn in so long that his lips became very sore and his notes were weak and off key. So, instead of playing, Louis sang along with the band in that deep, funny rough voice of his. The people liked his singing, so the owner said, "Your playing is no good but, anyhow, I'll keep you." He paid him fifty cents a night. At last Louis was a musician! Soon his lips became used to the horn again. He played so well after a while that other musicians came from all over New Orleans just to hear him.

Many dance band musicians in New Orleans then did not know how to read music. They learned by listening to each other's playing. Many white musicians, including Tom Brown and Jack Teagarden, liked the happy rhythms of black musicians. So they tried to learn them by listening to piano players like Jelly Roll Morton, or trumpet players like Buddy Bolden, King Oliver, and Bunk Johnson. In 1915 Tom Brown took a white band from New Orleans to Chicago. And in 1917 another all-white band called the Original Dixieland

Jass Band went to New York from New Orleans. For the first time the word "jazz" — then spelled "jass" — appeared in connection with the kind of music these men played.

Meanwhile, young Louis Armstrong began to play with a very good trombonist, Kid Ory. In the New Orleans Country Club and at the Tulane University dances, folks applauded loudly when Louis played his horn or sang his sad-funny blues. Soon a good pianist named Fate Marable asked Louis to play with his group on the S.S. "Sidney" running between New Orleans and St. Louis. Even though this was the first time young Louis had ever been far away from home, he enjoyed being part of the band that took New Orleans music up and down the river. Later Louis played on the S.S. "St. Paul" in Marable's Jaz-E-Saz Band. It had a wonderful drummer named Baby Dodds; a fine banjoist, Johnny St. Cyr; and the best bass player in New Orleans, Pops Foster. Louis became a better and better musician. When he left the riverboats in 1921, he became a part of Papa Celestin's Tuxedo Brass Band. This band played at all the best balls in New Orleans. A few months later the great King Oliver, whom Louis had admired so much when he was a little boy, sent for him to be a part of his orchestra at the Lincoln Garden in Chicago.

The Birth of Jazz

By this time the word "jazz" was known all across America. Louis Armstrong had been listening to it in New Orleans all his life but had never called it jazz. Now people everywhere wanted to hear this kind of music.

Nobody knows just how that name for Dixieland music

LOUIS ARMSTRONG (THIRD FROM RIGHT) IS PLAYING
TRUMPET IN FATE MARABLE'S ORCHESTRA.

got started. Some say it came from a spasm band player whose name was Jasper — Jas, for short. Some say the boy's name was Charles, but that he wrote it abbreviated to Chas. Certainly some of the first bands to use the word spelled it with an "s" or a double "s" — "jas" or "jass." (People who could not read very well pronounced "Chas." as "chaz" or "jaz.") Others say that in New Orleans, in about 1900, there was a band called Razz's Band, and that somehow the name of this band got changed to Jazz Band. Others say the word "jazz" had an African origin. Anyhow, by the time Louis Armstrong got to Chicago, folks were calling all Dixieland bands jazz bands, and their new music was called jazz.

To Louis, of course, it was not new music. It was just his old familiar music with a new name. It was the music that he heard Buddy Bolden play in the marching bands when he was a child. It was the music he plunked out on his little cigar box, Jelly Roll's ragtime, the blues his mother hummed, the spirituals his grandmother crooned, and the drumbeats his great-grandmother told him she heard in Congo Square. All of this was woven into the way he and Fate Marable, Baby Dodds, and Pops Foster played on the riverboats. When Louis stood up in front of a great crowd of people in Chicago and played his cornet, his music came out of these memories. And it was different from any other music most people had ever heard. It was fun. And it was jazz.

JAZZ IS FUN

Improvising

The tunes most of the old New Orleans jazz musicians played came directly from memory. These songs were long-familiar melodies and rhythms they had heard all their lives — melodies and rhythms which were African, French, Spanish, and Creole. They could play them together, weaving one rhythm against the another, without any trouble. Once they had heard a tune by ear, they did not need any written music. It was fun to improvise — to play a piece differently almost each time they played, partly composing as they went along. It was also fun to make new little breaks between the musical phrases. Since it was no fun playing exactly the same thing over and over, they made up riffs, runs, and the sliding notes called glissandos to suit the way a person felt at each different playing. When you felt very happy, you might play "hot." When you felt sad, you might play "deep" blues. This meant repeating the sad old weary tune over and over, but making each chorus different. Also, each phrase was changed a little and sometimes a new ending was composed.

Jazz first began with thousands and thousands of people whose names nobody remembers anymore. These people were the drummers in Congo Square and the rivermen along the Mississippi. They were the musicians in the marching bands of New Orleans and the singers of spirituals in country churches. Minstrels, children beating out rhythms on washboards and tin tubs, and the people living on plantations who made up a field holler or a blues contributed to what we now call jazz. The piano player who could not read music playing a tune — teasing it, "ragging" it, having a "rag time" — and the untrained musicians bringing their instruments together on street corners or in lodge halls played their part too. That is how jazz was born. And it was not just playing music. It was playing — like a game — playing with music, for fun.

That is what made jazz new and different. Most trained musicians play the notes of a piece the same way each time. But an old-time jazz musician might play a piece a little differently each time. Jazz came to be known as a playfully happy music. Even the sad old blues had, beneath the blue melodies, a steady rolling beat that seemed to be marching somewhere to something better, something happy. So, when Louis Armstrong lifted his trumpet to his mouth in Chicago, people there were happy. When he sang the blues, they were sad and happy at the same time. And when Louis sang "scat" style—"skee-daddle-de-dee-daddle," meaning nothing — people laughed until they almost split their sides. Jazz is happy!

Syncopation

One of the things that makes jazz a happy music is its continuous syncopation — its use of surprising offbeats — and its interweaving of rhythms, one over the other. Jazz rhythms are not always simple. A march is a straight 4/4 beat such as a regular brass band plays. But when jazz began to win acceptance, the New Orleans bands started playing one rhythm against another, or sometimes several rhythms against each other. In jazz there are usually at least two rhythms going at once. One part of the music keeps a steady beat. The other part, however, dodges the accent, plays around with the time, and creates syncopated counterrhythms against a 4/4 beat. It jumps ahead or holds back, anticipates or retards — skips — hits — and misses — weaving together many rhythms, called polyrhythms. But all of it forms a teasing happy combination that rolls along smoothly and merrily. It is this gay going ahead, this rippling, dancing drive, in and out and around the beat, that makes jazz.

Melodies in jazz do the same things. While a cornet plays the tune, the clarinet may play a countermelody — that is, one melody against the other. But off notes, blue notes, glides, slurs, and slides are common in jazz. The five-tone scale, frequent seventh and ninth chords, and the melody patterns of the twelve-bar blues are often used. The early jazz bands used chord combinations that no one had ever heard in European music. This "close" harmony, sometimes above the melody, like the "barbershop chords" of singing, is common in jazz. The brasses and reeds of jazz are singing instruments and are often used as if they were voices.

CHICAGO AND NEW YORK

A teen-age schoolboy named Bix Beiderbecke used to come to the Lincoln Garden in Chicago to hear Louis. Bix later be-

BIX BEIDERBECKE, A FAMOUS HORN PLAYER,
TAUGHT HIMSELF TO PLAY THE CORNET.

came a great horn-blower himself. Art Hodes, Mezz Mezzrow, and other young musicians like Jimmy McPartland also
came to hear Louis. In New Orleans and in Chicago, musicians learned from each other. To the Chicago boys this new
Dixieland music was a wonderful and exciting thing. They
began to try to play like the men from the Deep South.
When the Original Dixieland Band moved on to New York,
Broadway musicians began to try to play the same way. In
1921 King Oliver and his Creole Jazz Band had toured the
West Coast, and so, from California to New York, jazz began
to go everywhere.

In 1924 Paul Whiteman and his orchestra gave a famous
jazz concert at Aeolian Hall in New York. He introduced for
the first time the "Rhapsody in Blue" by the young composer
George Gershwin. There were no black players in Paul
Whiteman's Orchestra. But George Gershwin's "Rhapsody in
Blue" (one of the earliest attempts at putting jazz into concert form) opened with the upward wail of a clarinet glis-
sando and went into an echo of the sad old blues of the
Deep South. Jazz had begun to influence serious music.
Classical composers like Igor Stravinsky used jazz effects.
This jazz-classical combination is known as "Third Stream
Music," a term coined by Gunther Schuller, who composes
symphonies, ballets, and jazz sonatas. Stravinsky, Ravel, Car-
penter, and Copland have all recognized its power. The
famous American conductor Walter Damrosch once said,
"Lady Jazz, adorned with her intriguing rhythms, has danced
her way around the world, even to the northern Eskimos and
the South Sea Polynesians."

Now jazz concerts are often held in Carnegie Hall,

where at one time only symphonies were heard. So from the Congo to Carnegie, from New Orleans to New York, and from New York to the whole world went the rhythms of African drums.

WHAT IS JAZZ?

Before 1900 many musicians, conductors, and composers in America had been born in Europe and had come to our country as immigrants. Naturally much of our music, both popular and classical, was then greatly influenced by European music and followed its styles and forms. Strangely enough, in those days, too, many Americans thought that if singers or musicians did not come from Europe they could not be very good. If songs did not sound like German Lieder, or dance pieces were not Viennese waltzes or mid-European mazurkas or polkas, many Americans thought they did not amount to very much. Many of our most famous composers of theater music had also been born abroad. Victor Herbert was from Ireland, Sigmund Romberg from Hungary, Rudolf Friml from Czechoslovakia. Irving Berlin, who wrote "Alexander's Ragtime Band," is from Russia. These composers writing for America were nevertheless influenced by the musical styles of Europe. People enjoyed their music, but much of it was not especially American. It did not grow out of American soil. It was not until ragtime, the blues, and particularly jazz came along that America had a music we could call our very own to play and sing.

The ragtime players, blues singers, and brass band marchers whose music combined to produce jazz were all born in America. The continuous mounting syncopations of jazz were born here. Europeans used syncopation in their music, but not very much. The Africans used a very complex syncopation in their music, but they did not combine it with melody and harmony the way Americans did. And they never had the many different instruments we use. They didn't have cornets, slide trombones, pianos, or clarinets. The way Americans began to syncopate those instruments as they played them became very much a part of jazz.

Jazz is a way of playing music even more than it is a composed music. Almost any music can become jazz if it is played with jazz treatment. In New Orleans there were syncopated marches and ragtime waltzes. Paul Whiteman jazzed Rimski-Korsakov's "Song of India." Ornette Coleman was called a "jazzhound" when he was dismissed from his high school band because he jazzed up the "Washington Post March." Maxine Sullivan became famous by singing "Loch Lomond," not as it came from Scotland, but as she felt it, jazz style.

"Loch Lomond" (Straight version)

"Loch Lomond" (Swing version)

The Swingle Singers dared to swing Bach — and even devoted listeners of classical music loved it. Nobody knows on what levee the first blues song was sung. Today blues have become jazz songs. The off-beat rhythms of ragtime and blues are jazz.

JAZZ INSTRUMENTS

Folks in New Orleans paid so much attention to players like old Buddy Bolden, King Oliver, and young Louis Armstrong because they were trumpeters and the trumpet was the leading instrument in their bands. The other brass instrument was a slide trombone. The reed instrument was a clarinet. Drums, banjo or guitar, tuba, or maybe a string bass were the percussion that provided the basic rhythm. Pops Foster threw away his bow and plucked the bass with his fingers. This is the way most bass viols are played in jazz today. There was no piano in the early Dixieland bands. But when King Oliver moved northward, in Chicago he added a piano. Lil Hardin, who later became Louis Armstrong's wife, played it. It was fashionable in the North for all the jazz bands to have a piano. Besides, printed music was beginning to be used for jazz, and often it was only the pianist who could read printed music — most early jazz musicians had very little education.

As jazz bands grew larger — from four or five players

HERE LIL HARDIN PLAYS THE PIANO
IN KING OLIVER'S DIXIELAND BAND.

to twelve or fifteen — the brass, reed, and rhythm sections were increased. Today, in the large bands, the brass instruments are usually trumpets and trombones; the reeds are alto and tenor saxophones and a clarinet; and the percussion is the piano, guitar, string bass, and drums.

In the old New Orleans jazz bands there were no saxophones. This instrument was invented in 1846 by a Belgian, Adolphe Sax. The saxophone was used mostly in military bands until Chicago and New York jazz bands took it up — at first just for comic effects. But with some of the northern bands it grew to be almost as important a serious solo instrument as the trumpet. For fun, some bands now have a great variety of percussion-makers besides drums. These are rattles, bells, blocks, coconut shells, and brushes.

Rumbas and other Caribbean dances introduced into our orchestras little double drums — the bongos; the claves (two sticks that are knocked together); the guiro (a calabash that is scraped); and the maracas (seed-filled gourds that are shaken). Caribbean music is very old music from Cuba, Haiti, and other islands of the Caribbean Sea. Its rhythms also go back to Africa, but they have now become a part of American jazz.

SWING MUSIC

When Louis Armstrong came to New York in 1924, he played with Fletcher Henderson's Orchestra at the Roseland

Ballroom on Broadway. This orchestra used written music, and most of its players had been trained in good music schools. So it was not easy for Louis to play with them. He was not used to just playing a piece. Instead, he played with it and, at the same time, improvised — making up the music as he went along — letting his fancy take flight. But by 1924 there were many reasons why the younger band leaders felt that jazz had to be written down on paper. For one thing, when records were made they always had to be the same length (about three minutes). And, when radio programs were arranged a few years later, they had to be timed to the split second. The bands also had to play things the same way and the same length when they played for shows in theaters. So "arrangers" were employed to arrange music exactly to suit these various needs. This written and arranged jazz — less wild, hot, strange, and exciting than the old New Orleans Dixieland jazz — gradually came to be called "swing" music. When it used a great many sentimental songs for its melodies, it was called "sweet" jazz.

Louis Armstrong's wife Lil helped him learn to read music better and to understand written arrangements quickly. In a little while, just as he had been a star of the old Dixieland groups, Louis became a star of the new swing bands. No matter what kind of band Louis played in, his trumpet sang out. Broadway liked Louis. Ted Lewis, Paul Whiteman, and the former schoolboy who had listened often to him in Chicago, Bix Beiderbecke, all were at the Roseland to hear him and to study his style. On the West Coast many other young musicians heard Louis at the Cotton Club in Hollywood. Louis made hundreds of records and often played on the radio. In the years that followed, Armstrong's once-improvised riffs, breaks, and solos became a part of modern American jazz.

Many good swing orchestras developed before World War II, some playing "sweet" and some playing "hot." Duke Ellington, Glen Gray, Benny Goodman, Red Nichols, Glenn Miller, Vincent Lopez, Cab Calloway, Bunny Berigan, Charlie Barnet, Jimmy Lunceford, Artie Shaw, Woody Herman, Bennie Moten, Tommy Dorsey, and Count Basie all had bands that millions of people enjoyed. Louis Armstrong, too, had his own band. And he traveled almost all over the world playing jazz from the Palladium in London to the great halls of Tokyo. When big bands were no longer so popular, and many smaller jazz band combinations were formed, Louis had one of the best, with both white and black musicians playing together: Earl Hines, piano; Jack Teagarden, trombone; Barney Bigard, clarinet; Cozy Cole, drums; and Arvell Shaw, bass. From Chicago to Copenhagen they played jazz.

DUKE ELLINGTON

Duke Ellington has always shared honors with Louis Armstrong in jazz history. The Duke formed a band in 1918 and kept it going for fifty-six years. Although he was a gifted pianist, his arranger Billy Strayhorn said, "His real instrument is his band." The Duke was a master at swing and had his

DUKE ELLINGTON SHARES HONORS WITH
LOUIS ARMSTRONG IN JAZZ HISTORY.

own special style — soft, mellow tones and velvety melodies — "the Ellington effect."

He was one of America's greatest jazz composers. His first piece was "Soda Fountain Ragtime," which he wrote when he was a fourteen-year-old soda fountain clerk. Many of his songs are classics. He composed more than a thousand songs, symphonic suites, jazz concertos, and sacred jazz church music. The Duke played and composed for symphony orchestras. (Toscanini commissioned him to write "Harlem," a suite for orchestra.)

When he took his sixteen-piece band to Europe, Ellington was treated like a true duke. Leningrad acclaimed him. France decorated him with its highest award, the Legion of Honor, and he played before the queen of England at her request.

When Ellington was seventy years old, President Nixon had a birthday party for him at the White House. His gift was the Presidential Medal of Freedom, our highest award.

Ellington had been at the White House before, when he was a little boy. He visited his father, who worked there as a butler!

NEW FORMS OF JAZZ

Bebop
In the 1940s, while the swing bands made money playing at college proms and high society dances, a kind of jazz called

bebop was born. Some talented black musicians working in small night spots exploded with sounds and rhythms that were new. The word "bebop" was used to describe the harsh sounds and shifting accents of the music.

Bebop, usually called bop, was nothing one could sing or whistle. Many bop pieces were based on the notes of old jazz tunes like "I've Got Rhythm." Boppers just played around with the notes of the melody when they improvised. They created complicated rhythms and harmonies. Bebop could only be played by the most brilliant musicians. Dizzy Gillespie blew bebop on his trumpet. Pianists Thelonious Monk and Bud Powell, drummer Max Roach, and saxophone players Lester Young and Charlie Parker had jam sessions. They created a new emotion-packed jazz that only the most serious listener could appreciate.

Bebop was played by small groups. Talented soloists made this music great. When musicians were not playing solo they would "feed" the soloist by just hitting occasional chords for background accompaniment. Great horn players like Charlie Parker would be given lots of "blowing room" — or time to improvise. Parker often played a forty-five-minute solo. He was one of the greatest jazz musicians in history.

Bop players wanted to show that they were different from conventional musicians who played in dance bands. Boppers seemed to ignore the audience. They often walked away after performing only a half-hour solo. Sometimes boppers played with their backs to listeners. They would not cater to society. Some musicians defied the establishment by wearing odd costumes or sporting goatees and dark glasses.

DURING A JAM SESSION, MUSICIANS IMPROVISE
AND EXPERIMENT WITH DIFFERENT RHYTHMS AND
HARMONIES — THEY REALLY HAVE A GOOD TIME.

They were different, and many people did not like their music or their personalities. But their genius at improvising was talked about. Small bands soon took up the new bebop riffs, chords, and bongo drumbeats.

Cool Jazz

Sometime in the 1950s when the bebop wave passed, a style called "cool" or "progressive" jazz took over. It was a reaction against the loud, hot, wild sounds of bop.

Cool was a new way of playing. It was restrained and understated. The performers were dignified and serious. Perhaps they were anxious to show the world that bop mannerisms were not used by all black jazz players.

Cool, played by small groups, introduced clashing chords that were not used in the older forms of jazz. The cool musicians brought in a relaxed lag-along style, playing after the beat.

Trumpeter Miles Davis made cool popular. He is one of jazz history's greats because he developed this new style of music. Saxophonists Gerry Mulligan and Stan Getz and bass player Charlie Mingus also shaped the cool way of playing.

Cool was usually played by small jazz bands, called "combos." But the big bands of Stan Kenton and Woody Herman also adapted this new style. Cool was calm and soft. It brought the flute, the French horn, and the oboe into the jazz scene. These instruments, usually part of symphony orchestras, added new tone colors to jazz. There were even bagpipers that played cool jazz.

Sometimes cool was played like classical music. The Modern Jazz Quartet, led by pianist John Lewis, played written scores that were almost classical in form. (A score is the copy of a musical composition in written or printed form.) Another group, formed by pianist Dave Brubeck, experimented with European rhythms, such as a "jazz waltz." These groups toured the world playing this chamber music jazz to packed houses in concert halls.

Jazz Rock

Musicians who played cool did not expect people to dance to their music. Then in the 1950s rock took over the teenage world. It started feet moving to a hard, steady beat. Rock 'n' roll pounded its rhythms loud, with the help of hi-fi amplifiers and electric guitars. The beat was heard more than the melody. Kids jumped and danced and screamed with an excitement that no cool could inspire. They did the twist to Chubby Checker's music. They cried and fainted when rock hero Elvis Presley sang. And they drove their parents wild playing the early Beatles records. The booming beat that was deafening noise to adults was beautiful music for teen-agers. Rock groups grew rich because their high-energy music appealed to an enormous audience of young people.

But is rock jazz? Most critics don't think so. Pure rock does not have musicians who improvise. Improvisation is basic to jazz. And the heavy, solid beat of electrified instruments so essential in rock 'n' roll is not a part of jazz.

However, jazz rock, or "progressive rock," developed in the late 1960s. Much of the credit goes to Miles Davis, the brilliant trumpet player who had introduced cool to many people. He put some rock beat into his jazz. And his group started to use electrified instruments. Because he is a respected leader in the jazz world, other groups imitated him.

MILES DAVIS IS CREDITED WITH
INTRODUCING "JAZZ ROCK" TO MANY PEOPLE.

For example, Billy Cobham and Weather Report played a blend of this combination of jazz and rock. And Blood, Sweat and Tears, the first commercial band to play this type of music successfully, had soloists who knew how to improvise. The Mahavishnu Orchestra, led by guitarist John McLaughlin, also attracted crowds of jazz and rock fans.

Even though electric pianos and guitars are now used by jazz groups, and reeds and brasses are heard in rock bands, there is still a gulf separating jazz from rock.

Free-Form Jazz

A new kind of jazz called "Free-Form" or the "New Thing" came on the scene in the 1960s.

It was free and new, all right. Musicians broke all the rules. Two or more players improvised at the same time. There were no laws of harmony. Any note could be played with any other note. There wasn't any set rhythm, musical scale, or key to follow. The musician played whatever came to mind. Free-form meant no form at all.

Ornette Coleman was the leader of this radical jazz. He is a musical genius who walked a long, hard road before anyone noticed him. Ornette's father died when he was seven years old. The family was so poor that Ornette had little hope of ever owning a musical instrument. He was grateful that he could borrow a cousin's saxophone once in a while. He also borrowed a music book from school in order to teach himself to play.

Then on the morning of his fifteenth birthday, Ornette's mother told him to look under his bed. He found her gift to him — a saxophone.

Within a year Ornette was so good that he played with a few bands. He worked his way from his home in Texas to the West Coast by playing jazz. He also worked as a carnival hand and an elevator operator so that he could earn money to study music and harmony.

Then, in 1959, Coleman was featured in a New York nightclub playing a cheap white plastic saxophone. He introduced a style of jazz that broke all musical rules. Angry jazz fans hooted at him and some tried to chase him off the bandstand. He was criticized for playing out of tune and for not knowing anything about harmony. Coleman's answer to that was "You can play sharp in tune or flat in tune." He continued the "New Thing," even though many people refused to consider his playing acceptable.

But Coleman was appreciated by a small group of followers. One of them said that Ornette was reaching for a sound never heard yet. Ornette's explanation for his radical style was "I play pure emotion."

Today Ornette Coleman is one of the great musicians in the jazz world. He keeps experimenting with new compositions and new effects. He may play the same music night after night, but he plays it differently each time.

John Coltrane, a brilliant saxophonist who studied Coleman's style, was another free jazz artist. One critic remarked that he played his saxophone "as if he were determined to blow it apart." Coltrane's style was an important influence on all modern jazz. He used Arabic and Indian harmonies in his music. During long solos that often lasted forty-five minutes, Coltrane produced different sounds using new chords and a variety of different scales.

ORNETTE COLEMAN INTRODUCED
"FREE-FORM" JAZZ — A STYLE
THAT BROKE ALL MUSICAL RULES.

Free-form jazz has been compared with abstract painting — another art medium where old rules were broken for a new effect. Like abstract painting, free jazz is an admired art form today.

A JAZZ-HAPPY WORLD

We have seen that jazz takes many forms — blues, swing, pop, cool. Everything from Dixieland to free-form is played today. One kind of jazz doesn't knock out an earlier style. The whole history of jazz is alive and playing well. Luckily, most of the important jazz musicians, like Jelly Roll Morton, Armstrong, Bessie Smith, and Ellington, have recorded their music, so they will always be able to entertain us.

Jazz is a popular American export. Count Basie took it to Europe; Benny Goodman sounded out Asia; Louis Armstrong visited Africa; and Dizzy Gillespie brought his talents to South America.

Our musicians absorbed and imported music from foreign countries. One can hear the beat of African tribal drums, the wail of mid-Eastern music, and the tone of the Indian sitar in today's jazz.

Jazz has become recognized as a great American art form. It is taught for credit in hundreds of universities. Special jazz festivals are staged in countries all over the world — even in Communist Poland and Russia, where jazz was once illegal. The world is jazz-happy.

GLOSSARY

Arranger. The person who writes down what voices and instruments are used in a musical composition.

Ballad. A simple song.

Beat. Rhythm and the tempo or timing in music.

Blowing Room. A time for horn players to play alone and improvise.

Blue Notes. Slurred notes somewhere between flat and natural notes.

Boogie-woogie. A kind of blues that is played on the piano with a strong, deep bass added.

Brass. Musical instruments of the trumpet or horn family, usually made of brass.

Break. A very brief passage between musical phrases — often improvised in unwritten jazz. Armstrong was famous for his breaks.

Chord. A combination of notes that blend and sound good when played together.

Classical Music. Music of lasting beauty. It includes musical forms such as chamber music, opera, and symphony. It does not include folk, popular, or jazz music.

Close Harmony. Harmony in which three upper notes of a chord lie within an octave (a series of eight notes).

Combo. A small jazz or dance band.

Counter Melody. Playing one melody against the other.

Cutting Contest. Musicians who got together and tried to outplay each other had cutting contests. One musician would cut in and play solo, after another musician played solo.

Feed. Musicians "feed" a soloist when they just play a few chords in the background.

Glissando. A rapid sliding up or down the musical scale.

Harmony. A pleasing arrangement of simultaneous sounds.

Hymn. A song in praise of God.

Improvisation. Music composed while it is being played. It may also be new variations on an old theme. A musician is judged in jazz by his or her ability to improvise.

Jam Session. Holding a jam session, "jamming," means getting together to play jazz.

Jazz Concerto. A jazz composition for one or more soloists accompanied by an orchestra.

Jubilee. A black folk song that tells about future happiness.

Key. The tonality of a scale.

Key Note. The first note on the scale used in a musical composition.

Melody. A musical phrase or song. A tune.

Minstrel. An entertainer who sang songs, told jokes, and did imitations. Usually white entertainers blackened their faces and became black minstrels.

Minstrel Bones. Polished animal bones that were held between the fingers and shaken to make a dancing rhythm.

Musical Scale. A graduated series of musical tones going up or down.

Percussion. This is the beat of a musical instrument. The drums provide jazz with its basic beat, but the banjo or guitar, the string bass or tuba, and the piano also provide percussion. Any or all of these instruments may make up the rhythm section of a jazz band. Chords may be used as a beat to create harmonized percussion.

Phrase. A short musical thought, usually two to four measures long.

Quadrille. A square dance for four couples. Also, the music for this dance.

Ragtime. Rhythm with a syncopated melody and a regularly accented accompaniment.

Reed. A hollow wind instrument. A small piece of cane or metal attached to the mouthpiece vibrates to make sounds. (The oboe and clarinet are examples.) The first reed instruments were hollow stalks of grass.

Rhythm. A part of music with accent, tempo, or time. In jazz, rhythm is not limited to percussion beats. Volume, tone, and pitch may also be used to give a jazz performance accents of sound rhythm.

Riff. A single rhythmic phrase repeated over and over. It can be background for a melody, or it may be used as a main melody. Riffs are developed by musicians. Brasses and reeds "riff" — they throw a phrase back and forth.

Score. Written or printed music.

Spiritual. A religious song developed among Southern blacks.

Sweet Jazz. Jazz that uses sentimental songs for its melodies.

Syncopation. This is a shifting of accents and stress from what are normally strong beats to the weak beats. It often means playing one rhythm against another in such a way that listeners want to move, nod heads, clap hands, or dance. Syncopation is part of jazz.

Tailgate. A style of jazz trombone playing, marked by the use of slides and held notes.

Third-Stream Music. Jazz and classical effects combined in a musical composition.

Tone Color. Jazz instruments may take on the varied tones of the singing or speaking voice in a variety of tonal colorations. At one time different instruments may be playing different melodies.

Tune. A succession of pleasing musical tones. A melody.

INDEX

Acknowledgments

For invaluable guidance concerning the history, development, artists, and materials of jazz music, the author is most grateful to the books, magazine articles, comments, or record notes on jazz by George Avakian, Rudi Blesh, Arna Bontemps, Sterling Brown, E. Simms Campbell, Leonard Feather, Sidney Finkelstein, Robert Goffin, John Hammond, W. C. Handy, W. E. Harper, Rex Harris, S. I. Hayakawa, Wilder Hobson, John Tasker Howard, Max Jones, Orrin Keepnews, Alan Lomax, Albert McCarthy, Mezz Mezzrow, Nestor R. Ortiz Oderigo, Frederick Ramsey, Jr., Winthrop Sargeant, Charles Edward Smith, Ezra Staples, Marshall W. Stearns, Jack Walker, and especially Louis Armstrong.

The author and publisher wish also to thank the Handy Brothers Music Co., Inc., of New York, and W. C. Handy for permission to use excerpts from his "St. Louis Blues" (page 17) and "Memphis Blues" (page 21), both held in copyright by the W. C. Handy Music Co., Inc.